The stunning geodesic cupola, transparent and reticular, by Emilio Pérez Piñero has become a symbol of the museum and, by extension, of Figueres, the painter's birthplace.

Dalí took an active role in setting up his museum. Contemplating the execution of the Palace of the Wind.

2 HISTORY

The process for creating the Theatre-Museum began in 1961. In 1968, through a council motion, it was decided to turn the old local theatre into the Dalí Museum. The following year the construction of the geodesic cupola was entrusted to Emilio Pérez Piñero. On the 26 of June 1970 the Government Cabinet passed the project. In 1970 a pre-inauguration ceremony took place. The rehabilitation was the responsibility of the architects Joaquim Ros de Ramis and Alexandre Bonaterra. During August and September 1973 the museum held an exhibition entitled *Dalí, his art in jewellery*. On the 28 of September 1974 it was officially opened.

The Dalí Theatre-Museum

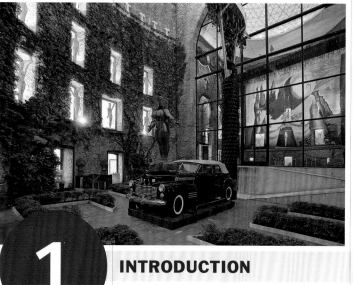

Spectacular view of the stalls and stage of the old theatre, with the *art déco* mannequins that welcome us to this centre full of suggestions.

"Start the house from the roof, like the great architects of the Renaissance, who imagined the cupola before anything else".
Salvador Dalí

1 INTRODUCTION

A singular space, a model for museums based on the conception of an artist to boost the semantic possibilities of his creation; an outstanding work, arranged in such a way as to give priority to the concepts and ideas over and above what is provided by chronologic historicism, and a distinct point of view, which all form part of what defines the Dalí Theatre-Museum of Figueres. In this total work, this great surrealist or ready-made object, Dalí distanced himself from the fashionable trends and provided a centre full of suggestions and provocations.

Mannequin
The *art déco* style gilded mannequins, actors of a mnemonic reference, with distinct attitudes, contrast in this space with heir cold and inexpressive presence.

Moving the Cadillac to its current position, the old theatre stalls.

Salvador Dalí on the Modernist sofa-display cabinet.

The artist in the space overlooked by the impressive painted ceiling that gives the name to the Palace of the Wind.

Dalí and Antoni Pitxot giving drawing classes on the old theatre stage, shortly after the museum was opened.

Monument dedicated to the Catalan philosopher Francesc Pujols, with allusions to science and to Ramon Llull.

Atom

The mannequins at the end of the central façade hold, in their arms raised towards the sky, a hydrogen atom, a constant reiteration of Dalí's passion for science.

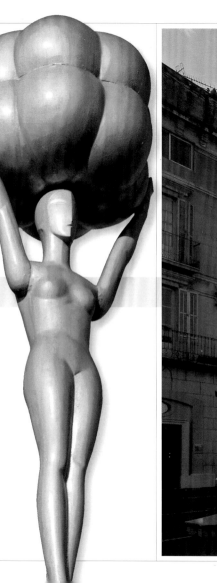

③ EXTERIOR

Introductory space in which Dalí alludes to some of his preferences and obsessions: science, with *Homage to Newton*, academic art, with the three sculptures in homage to Meissonier; more innovative art, with *The TV-Obelisk* by Wolf Vostell; and Catalan thought, with the monument in honour of Francesc Pujols. The building is crowned by mannequins, with crutches or loaves of bread over their heads. It is worth mentioning the figure of the diver, a symbol of immersion into the depths of the subconscious that await the visitor.

Mannequin with a gap in the solar plexus, with totally Dalinian symbols: the loaf of bread and the crutch.

Façade

Square and exterior of the Dalí Theatre-Museum, the old neo-classical city theatre designed by the architect Josep Roca i Bros in 1848.

Diver

Symbol of immersion into the depths of the subconscious that await the visitor.

Stone fountain that Dalí transforms into a lamppost and crowns with a reproduction of the hydrogen atom.

Installation by Salvador Dalí that complements the sculpture by Vostell.

Both Dalí and his muse wanted to have a presence on the outside of the Museum.

Obelisk

Upper part of the sculpture *The TV-Obelisk*, by Wolf Vostell, a monolith with fourteen televisions.

Homage to Meissonier

Jean Louis Ernest Meissonier, a pompier painter admired by Dalí. Sculpture produced by Antonin Mercié in 1895 and retouched by the painter, exhibited in 1979 in Paris for the *Dalí anthology exhibition*.

Plaça Gala-Salvador Dalí

Witness to the queues of visitors to the Museum, which Dalí liked so much.

Torre Galatea

The last residence of the painter and new extension of the museum. The old Casa Gorgot was "dalinised" with the eggs and *pa de crostons*, loaves of bread. Dalí was aware of other buildings, such as the Casa de las Conchas in Salamanca.

Eggs

The egg symbolises, for Dalí, birth, and fried eggs refer to intrauterine memories. Anything that is edible is fundamental in Dalí's work. As the artist himself stated, "Beauty will be edible or it will not be beauty".

Dalí intervenes on a mechanically reproduced image –the eye– and the whole piece provides the viewer with the impression of *cadavre exquis*.

4 VESTIBULE

This is a space of immersion into the Dalinian memory, since from the moment we enter we receive the keys and place the significant artists (Picasso, Miró, Antoni Pitxot, Gaudí, Gustave Moreau, Meissonier, Detaille, Ledoux or Carles Fages de Climent), people and movements –especially surrealism– and events of his career. Here there are also references to mythology, in the figure of Ganymedes, the Trojan hero. And of course, it could not be without a reference to Gala, his muse and wife, the representation of exclusive and reciprocal love.

Fan-collage
Produced by Amanda Lear under the supervision of Dalí.

Collage

Amanda Lear, under the supervision of Dalí, recovered the technique of collages. On this door they refer to the pictorial work of Dalí, with a high presence in international newspapers and magazines.

Eagle of Valls

Donation from the Xiquets de Valls, the Catalan *castellers* or human tower group, with the head of a Chinaman in the central opening of the breast, announcing the film by Dalí *Impresiones de Alta Mongolia*, 1975.

Ganymedes

Sculpture by José Álvarez Cubero with a gem-gilded helmet that came from the Russian Ballets. Ganymedes was the Trojan hero chosen by the Gods for his handsomeness to be the cupbearer of Zeus.

5 COURTYARD

This garden exposed to the sky is the old stalls section of the city theatre. It is dominated by the installation made up of the imposing Cadillac; the sculpture *The Great Esther* by Ernst Fuchs, which pulls, with its chains, the Trajan's column made of tyres; the marble bust of François Girardon and the "dalinised" *Slave* of Michelangelo, along with Gala's boat and a black umbrella, comprised, according to Dalí, the largest surrealist monument in the world. The whole piece takes on a Dionysian air: Dalí invites us to a ritual or game, the experience of our visit to the museum.

Rainy taxi
Created for the International Exhibition of Surrealism in Paris in 1938, organised by André Breton and Paul Éluard, with the cooperation of Marcel Duchamp.

Boat
The boat that Gala used in Portlligat, supported by crutches and the "dalinised" *Slave* of Michelangelo.

Automobiles

Symbols of modern life, youth, audacity and progress, and a constant in his work. They are complex machines that awaken all kinds of sentiments, as many perhaps as when contemplating classical beauty. The Cadillac and Rainy taxi were presented at the surrealist exhibition in Paris in 1938. The one in the Museum is a gift from the painter to Gala.

Stalls

At the end of the Spanish Civil War, the city theatre was burnt down and remained in disuse until Dalí decided to use the ruins of the building –we can see the burnt beams– for the future Dalí Museum. The old stalls are the museum's scenic space par excellence. Everything was designed and positioned in accordance with the artist's ideas, who also stated that one should never work by selection but by accumulation. Here the guidelines of the visit are outlined: the invitation to participate in a Dionysian festival.

Scenic view of
the stalls with the
Modernist lampposts
in the foreground, from
the Paris metro, by
Hector Guimard.

Mannequin
Art déco style
that welcomes
us to this centre.

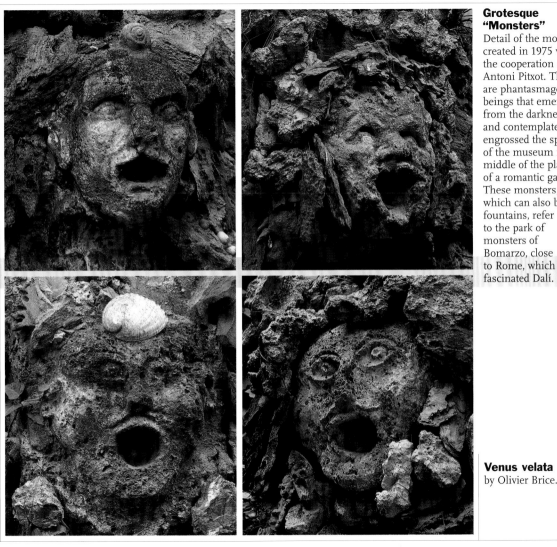

Grotesque "Monsters"

Detail of the monsters created in 1975 with the cooperation of Antoni Pitxot. They are phantasmagorical beings that emerge from the darkness and contemplated engrossed the spectacle of the museum in the middle of the plant life of a romantic garden. These monsters, which can also be fountains, refer to the park of monsters of Bomarzo, close to Rome, which fascinated Dalí.

Bas-relief of the "Arts and Trades" series, produced for the Universal Exhibition of Paris of 1900.

Venus velata
by Olivier Brice.

Roger freeing Angelica, also a clear reference to the myth of Saint George who slays the dragon to save the princess.

Sculpture of the group situated beneath the cupola.

6

CUPOLA

The stage of the old theatre, crowned by the stunning reticular and geodesic cupola, has become the symbol of the museums and by extension, of Figueres. Overlooking the stage is the enormous backdrop by Dalí produced for the ballet *Labyrinth*. We see the huge photographic oil painting in which, nude and seen from behind, Gala turns into the face of Abraham Lincoln, a reproduction of the *Halluconogenic Toreador* or the numerous installations, such as that of the *Christ Twisted*, in homage to Gaudí.

The Empordà skies also take on a leading role in the museum.

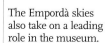

Labyrinth

View of the stage of the old theatre, with the tomb of Salvador Dalí. The Museum is a total work, his last great work, a theatre of the memory. On the left, a reproduction of the backdrop created for his ballet *Labyrinth*, 1941. In the background, the hands of creation, a reference to his admired master, Michelangelo.

Hercules pushing a column, c. 1977.

On the enormous canvas, beneath the central arch, we can see a double-image in which Gala, nude from behind, turns into the face of Abraham Lincoln. This is one of the many examples that show Dalí's interest in science, highly present in his final stage.

Folding mechanism by Emilio Pérez Piñero with Christ by Dalí.

El poll i la puça

(The louse and the flea), a sculpture in homage to two characters from his childhood who played –not particularly well– the barrel organ around the streets in exchange for a few coins.

Object found

According to Dalí, in the distant future this streetlight will be the most interesting object from the museum for archaeologists.

Bust of Beethoven, 1973, mixed technique. Dalí made it throwing live octopuses on the paper placed on the floor and used the graphics formed by the ink.

Gala nude looking at the sea which at 18 metres appears as President Lincoln, 1975, is homage to Mark Rothko, and the first example in painting of the use of digitalisation of the image, used here from a digital interpretation of the face of Lincoln obtained by the cybernetic scientist Leon D. Harmon.

7 TREASURE

Given this name by the painter, it is a room upholstered in red velvet, deliberately secluded, conceived like a casket, with some of the most important works in the museum and also the most charismatic for the artist. Featured among them is *The Basket of Bread*, an oil painting that represents the total enigma. Gala has an influential presence: the oil paintings *Gala from behind looking in an invisible mirror* or *Leda Atomica* are magnificent examples of this. The work is deliberately presented without any chronological order and sets out an interesting play of aesthetic and intellectual references.

The Spectre of Sex-Appeal, 1934.
In the lower right-hand part, a child Dalí, dressed as a sailor, looking at an enormous monster, soft and hard at the same time –which for him symbolised sexuality–, all framed within a hyperrealist Cap de Creus.

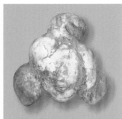

Bread

Bread is the most symbolically charged element in Dalí's work. In the surrealist stage it adopts, deliberately transgressor, a phallic meaning; in the classical stage it is a reflection of his obsession for form: "For six months my aim has been to recover the lost technique of the classical artists. It is the most rigorous from the point of view of geometric preparation". In the mystical-nuclear stage it possesses a Eucharistic value.

The Basket of Bread, 1945.
"This typically realist work is the one that has most satisfied my imagination".
S. Dalí

Stereoscopy
The right-hand part is based on *The Fire in the Borgo*, and the second part, on the left, on *The School of Athens*, both fresco paintings by Raphael.

Soft Self-portrait with Grilled Bacon, 1941. Dalí argued that the most consistent part of our representation is not the spirit or vitality, but the skin.

FISHMONGERS

It shows a series of works of distinct periods, without any kind of chronological order or standard, although the early and late periods dominate. It is worth mentioning works such as *Self-portrait with "L'Humanité"* or *Satirical Composition*, from 1923, and *Symbiotic Woman-Animal and Rotting Bird*, from 1928. Also, from the last period, works as evocative –and clearly referring to Michelangelo and Velazquez– as *Othello Dreaming Venice* or *Geological Echo*, from 1982. In the two central display cabinets are two examples of stereoscopy, a mechanical process in the optics of perception in the third dimension.

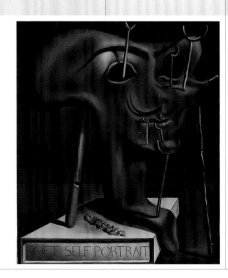

SOFT SELF PORTRAIT

Atom

According to Dalí, "the theory of atoms sees the world as a sponge of the sky", and from this comes the use of a reproduction of the hydrogen atom as a lamp. The artist stated that everything is in suspension in an atom and that in his atomic, or mystical-unclear period, he had to paint everything suspended in space.

Lilith

Installation-sculpture *Lilith-Homage* to Raymond Roussel, 1966, with double *Victory of Samothrace*. The French writer Raymond Roussel influenced the surrealists.

Illustrations for *Don Quixote* by Cervantes, 1946.
The genius of Cervantes sparks the genius of Dalí, and the meeting between the two gives rise to a series of images full of fantasy, magic, inventiveness and, in short, an imagination without limits.

9 CRYPT

A space corresponding to an early enlargement of the Museum, made up of three rooms. The first contains different drawings and watercolours. Then comes the "Dalí d'or" room, where there is a numbered series of medals on show and assembled in pieces of goldsmith work, with the double effigy of the painter and Gala. Finally we reach the crypt, with the tombstone made from Figueres stone, which bears the inscription "Salvador Dalí i Domenech. Marquis of Dalí of Púbol. 1904-1989", accompanied by six caduceuses from the same "Dalí d'or" series.

"And what is heaven? Where is it to be found? 'Heaven is to be found neither above nor below, neither to the right nor to the left, heaven is to be found exactly in the centre of the bosom of the man who has faith!'
At this moment I do not yet have faith, and I fear I shall die without heaven".
S. Dalí, *The Secret Life of Salvador Dalí*, 1942.

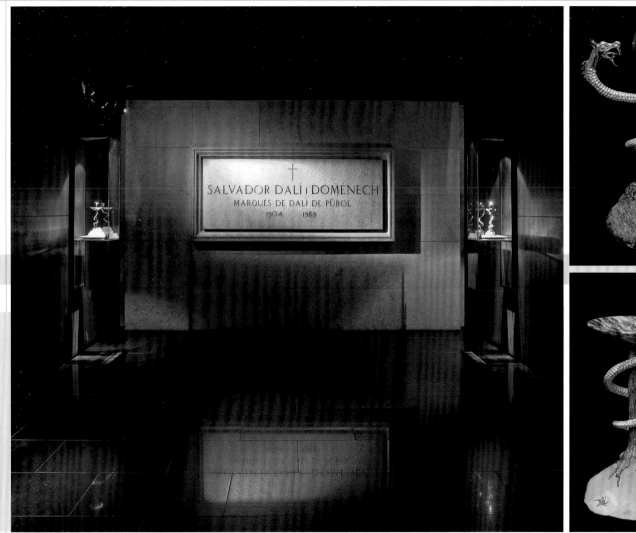

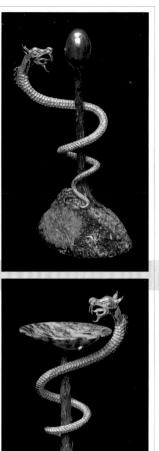

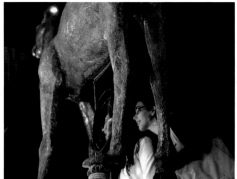

The lens
It shows us the three-dimensional nature of Mae West's face turned into a living room with sofa-lips.

MAE WEST

We can take in the three-dimensional application, the creation of a room, from a two-dimensional image, the wash on newspaper of *Face of Mae West which may be Used as an Surrealist Apartment*, c. 1934-35, which is on show in the Art Institute de Chicago. In order to be able to perceive this optical illusion, we have to go up a few steps crowned by a camel, from which a reducing lens is hanging and which provides us with the face of Mae West. We could even say that it is a forebear of pop art. In this room Dalí pays homage to the American hyperrealist painters.

Paradise

This installation can be associated with Marcel Duchamp or with another one by Dalí himself, for example *The Dream of Venus*.

Chair with spoons
Bronze sculpture designed by Salvador Dalí from a typical wicker chair.

Chair-mannequin, 1976. Sculpture, one of the Dalinian objects-assemblies full of accumulations, produced especially for this room.

Three examples of the complex Dalinian art, in which references to classical art and mythology combine with the most avant-garde tendencies.

Venus' Otorhinologic Head, 1964.

Venus de Milo with giraffe neck and drawers, 1973.

Head of Michelangelo, c. 1975.

Provocative Dalinian installation on the ceiling of the room. Another example of Dalí's desire to make the maximum use of space.

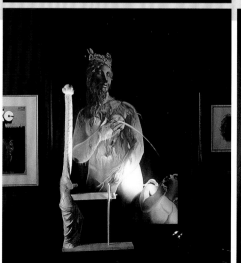

Drawers

One Dalinian image is that of the drawers that open at times in the human body. They are the drawers of the conscience. For Dalí, the figures with drawers represent the mystery of knowledge and the need to disseminate it. They are also homage to Sigmund Freud and the theory of psychoanalysis.

Bust of the retrospective woman, 1933, reconstructed in 1974.

Installation produced by Dalí which is based on a rotating concept, full of mystery, of the glances of the characters.

11

CORRIDORS

Ground floor

Lithographs from the series *Les songes drolatiques de Pantagruel*, 1973, fitted into four glass display cabinets, where Dalí presents installations in which he develops mystery, optical games and surrealists.

First floor

Outstanding here is the reproduction of the *Bust of the Retrospective Woman*, 1933. Dalí contributed to the invention of the surrealist object to a great extent. We also come across the *Venus de Milo with drawers* and the cabinet dedicated to Millet's Angelus, the work from which he created his well-known critical-paranoiac method.

Tristan and Isolde, 1945, used for one of the backdrops of the ballet *Mad Tristan.*

Critical-paranoiac method

Dalí defined it thus: "In truth I am no more than an automat that records, without judging, and as accurately as possible, the dictate of my subconscious: my dreams, the hypnagogic images and visions and all the concrete and irrational manifestations of the dark and sensational world discovered by Freud... The public must get pleasure from the unlimited resources of mysteries, enigmas and anxieties that such images offer the subconscious of the spectators".

Poetry of America or *The Cosmic Athletes*, 1943.
Produced during the American period, it is a forebear of the new cultural attitudes of the 20th century, especially of pop art.

Venus de Milo with drawers, 1936-64.

Entrance to the exhibition of work by Evarist Vallès.

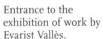

Lithograph from the series *Les songes drolatiques de Pantagruel*, 1973.

Allegory of the Memory, 1979. "Antoni Pitxot expresses, the sumptuousness of mineral silks and velvets". S. Dalí

12

SECOND & THIRD FLOORS

The second floor, at the express wish of Dalí, is dedicated permanently to the work of Antoni Pitxot. Of note here is the impressive *Allegory of the Memory*, which occupies the exact spot of the end of the corridor. On the floor we come across the Masterpiece Room, where we can see some works that Dalí collected over the years, from distinct periods and by different authors, alongside other creations of his, which he qualified "timeless masterpieces".

Masterpieces

It is in the Masterpiece Room where we can see, in a deliberately chosen chronological disorder, oil paintings that Dalí collected over time, along with his own works. On the right, one of his stereoscopic oil paintings. Also present are works by El Greco, Gerard Drou, Meissonier, Bouguereau, Fortuny, Urgell and Marcel Duchamp.

Saint Paul, by El Greco.

The court of the Alhambra, 1871. M. Fortuny.

Dalí from the back painting Gala from the back eternalized by six virtual corneas provisionally reflected by six real mirrors, 1972-73. S. Dalí.

General view, with the painted ceiling, of the *foyeur* of the old municipal theatre.

Bust of Velazquez Transforming itself into Three Talking Figures, 1974. A new example of double image, where a reproduction of *Las Meninas* stands out on the forehead.

13 PALACE OF THE WIND

In 1919 Dalí gave the first public exhibition of his work in this room. It is overlooked by the impressive painted ceiling that gives it its name. Dalí explained that this work was a paradox, which when the visitor looks up, they will see clouds, the sky and two suspended figures, but it is in reality a theatrical effect, since instead of the sky one sees the earth and, instead of the earth the sea. In the central part we can see the foreshortening of Gala and Dalí, who are pouring a shower of gold over Figueres and Empordà.

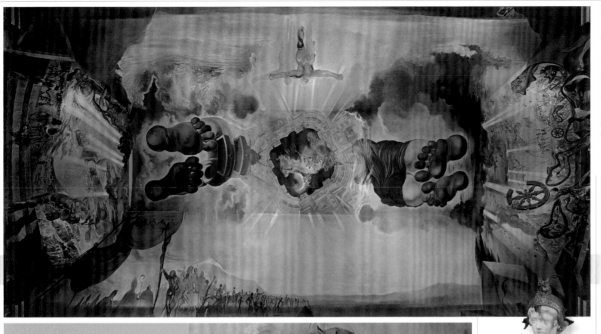

Impressive painted ceiling, *Palace of the Wind*, which gives its name to the room. The name comes from the poet Joan Maragall, who gave Empordà the name of "palace of the wind", referring to the Tramuntana.

Study for Galarina, 1943.

Soft/hard

A symbol that often appears in his work, it is an autobiographical representation. It is always a large head, with long eyelashes and a large nose. In this case it is a distinguished, hallowed artist in apotheosis.

Warrior on a pedestal formed by two Victories of Samothrace joined back to front.

Bedroom

Dalí conceived the whole room like his rooms: the bedroom, in the image, features the stunning tapestry *The Persistence of Memory*.

L'Empordà

The plain of Empordà painted by Dalí on the back of the Modernist sofa-display cabinet.

Ecstasy

"*Mystical ecstasy is super-happy, explosive, disintegrating, supersonic, undulating and corpuscular, ultra-gelatinous*".
S. Dalí

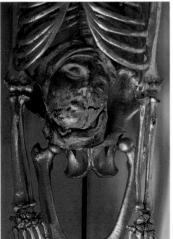

Surrealist Object Functioning Symbolically, 1931, reconstructed in 1974. Dalí spoke of it in his article "Objets surréalistes" for the magazine *Le surréalisme au service de la révolution*.

Bibendum

With head and neck of a swan. Another example of the fusion that the artist made between high culture and mass culture.

The Studio

Dalí dedicated this room, which he called his studio, to the symbol of the eternal female. In the foreground, the hyperrealist sculpture by John de Andrea, with a backdrop of the town of Cadaqués by Meifrèn.

Espadrille

Catalan footwear, used regularly by Dalí and incorporated into his iconographic universe.

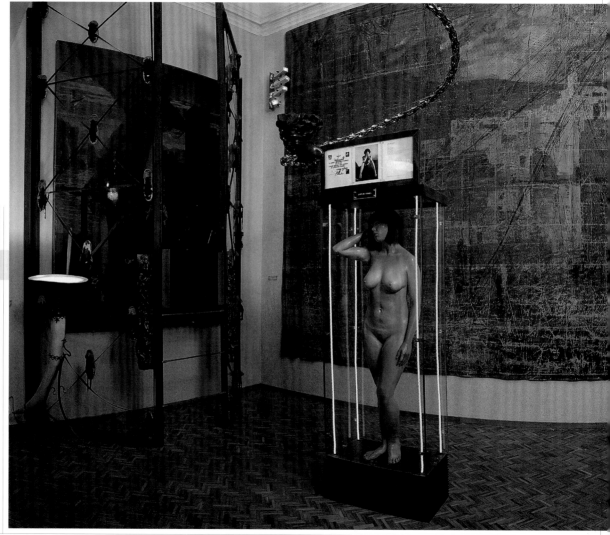

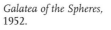
Galatea of the Spheres,
1952.

Lamp with
Modernist head of
the goddess Fortuna
that, with the eyes
bandaged snakes its
way down from the
ceiling in a chain
of spoons.

*Potrait of Gala with
Rhincerotic Symptoms,*
1954.

Hologram
*Holos! Holos!
Velázquez! Gabor!*
c. 1972-73.
According to Dalí,
since Velazquez' time,
all artists have been
interested in three-
dimensional realism.

The presence of Sigmund Freud and his interpretation of dreams could not be missing from his museum. Dalí wanted to perpetuate the memory of the interview he had with Freud in London (1938).

Installation overlooked by a large folding glass display cabinet, at the foot of which is the *Cybernetic Princess* (which we can see in detail on the right).

14 TORRE GALATEA

New extension of the museum, a more austere space and more in line with more conventional museum protocol, where we can see the Optical Illusions Room –remember that Dalí, since his childhood, loved the effects related to sight– and the purchases made by the Fundació Gala-Salvador Dalí and the last creations by the artist. It is in fact the artist's very last oil painting, *Untitled. Swallow's Tail and Cellos* (Catastrophe Series), from 1983, that bids us farewell from the museum and accompanies us towards the exit stairway.

Folding glass cabinet, the result of the collaboration between Dalí and the architect Emilio Pérez Piñero. Model of the project –never undertaken– for the door that leads to the stage from the courtyard.

Shrine

Replica of *Bramante's Shrine* where jewels designed by Dalí In the 1970s are exhibited, of which we could highlight the *Christ of Limpias*, c. 1970.

Optical illusions

Room dedicated to optical illusions and effects related to the sight, with the definition of images from the indefinite, which is time.

Babaouo

Scenic case with glass panels painted in oils.

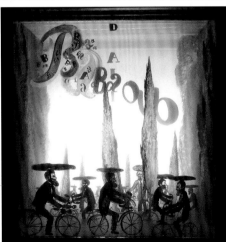

The Chair, 1975
Large-format stereoscopic work.

Stereoscopy

"Stereoscopy immortalises and legitimises geometry, since thanks to it we possess the third dimension of the sphere".
S. Dalí, *Ten recipes for immortality*.

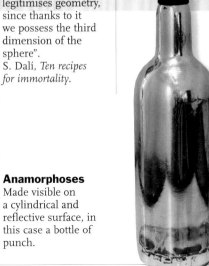

Since his childhood, Dalí had felt a passion for the optical effects related to the sense of sight and, in order to obtain a special perception of the sensitive world, combined and adapted artistic technique with the most advanced scientific technology of the time.

Anamorphoses

Made visible on a cylindrical and reflective surface, in this case a bottle of punch.

Night

In July and August you can visit the museum at night and have glass of Peralada pink cava.

The Chalice of Life, 1965. An electronic piece of jewellery that represents the chalice of Saint Teresa of Avila.

Apotheosis of the Dollar, 1965, a compendium of the most significant images, myths and obsessions that accompanied Dalí throughout his life.

15 JEWELS

In 1999 the Fundació Gala-Salvador Dalí acquired the collection of jewels designed by Dalí that had belonged to the American Owen Cheatham collection, and were given a new space, deliberately dark, in which we are shown both the jewels and the splendid preparatory drawings. Dalí explained that without a public these jewels would not fulfil their function: to give pleasure to the sight, extol the spirit, awaken the imagination and express convictions. The spectator therefore becomes the final artist and gives them life.

Pax Vobiscum, 1968.

The Royal Heart, 1953.
Piece of electronic jewellery.
"The rubies that beat represent the queen, whose heart throbs constantly for her people".
S. Dalí

The Space Elephant, 1961.

Cap de Creus

DALINIAN TRIANGLE

Salvador Dalí was an artist linked to his
landscape, integrated into it; he formed part
of it: "I am the Cap de Creus", he stated.
Therefore, to understand his imagination
we should visit the three centres that make
up the Dalinian Triangle: the house at
Portlligat, his only stable residence, with
the studio where he conceived and created
a large part of his work and in which he
soaked up the light and scenery of Cap de
Creus; the castle of Púbol, which he gave to
Gala, and in which he lived from 1982 until
1984; and finally, his Theatre-Museum in
Figueres.

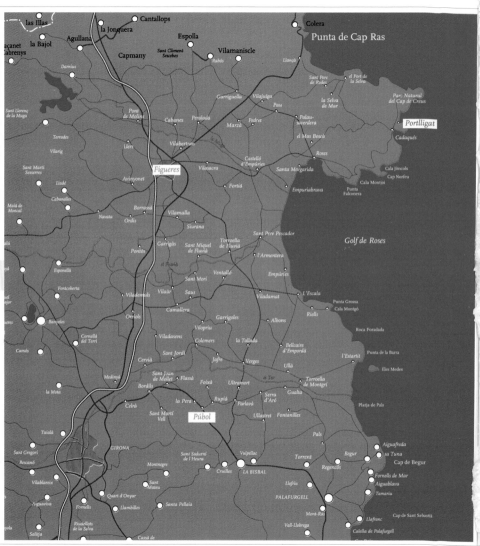